W0081515

I AM MY NAME

Na'kuset & Judith Henderson   Illustrated by **Onedove**

Alfred A. Knopf 🐕 New York

When my sister was six,
I was three.
She watched over me
and tried to keep me safe.

We were alone that night.
Curled up.
Twined together like a braid.
Arms enfolding. Hands holding.

There was a
Knock
Knock
Knock
at the door.

My sister opened it.
Flashlight people.
They whispered.
"Shhh. It will be all right."
They lifted us. Like feathers.

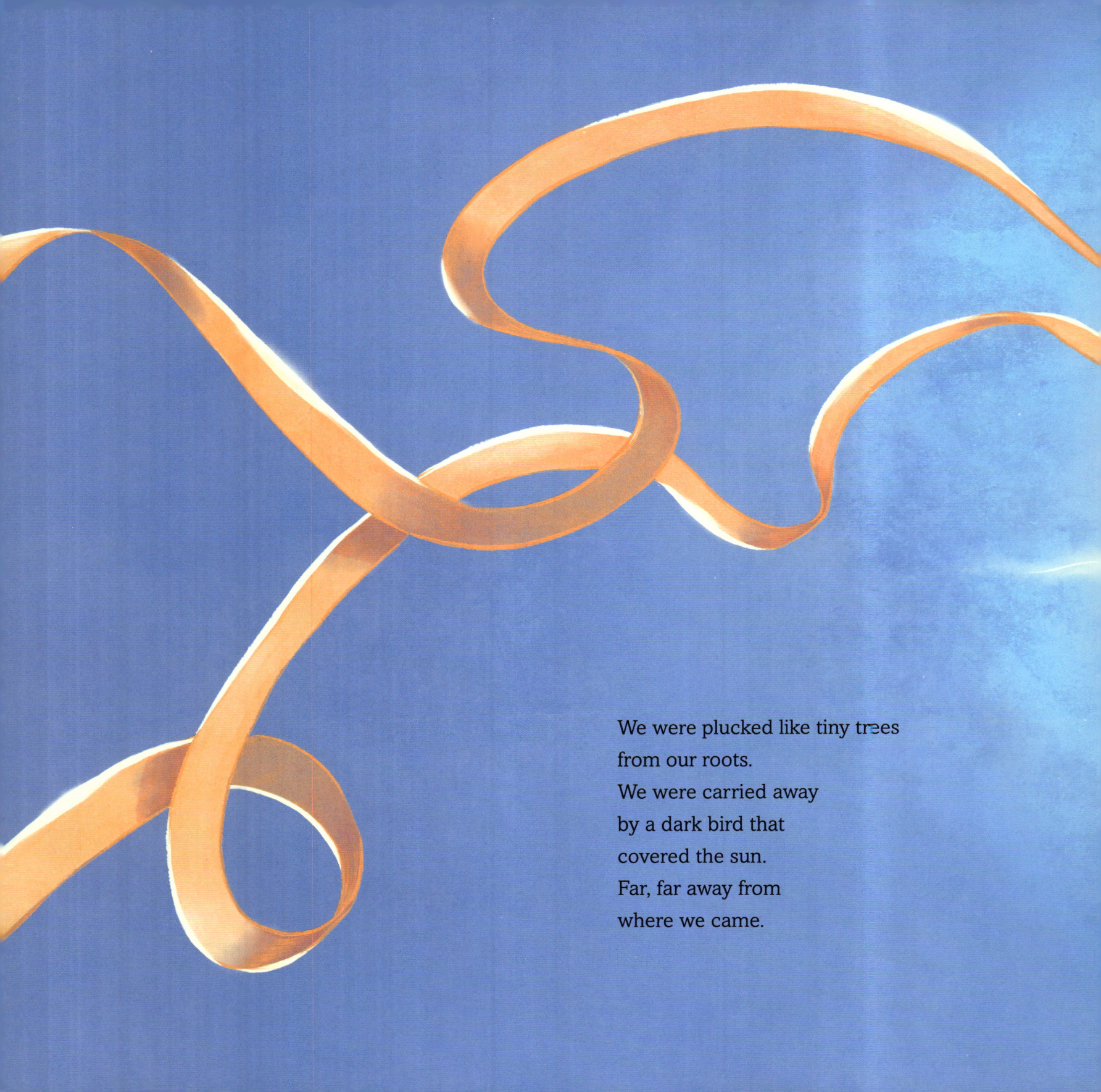

We were plucked like tiny trees
from our roots.
We were carried away
by a dark bird that
covered the sun.
Far, far away from
where we came.

I dream.
I dream of flying.

When I open my eyes,
I am in a room of pink and white.
There is a bear.
It is pink and white too.
But where is my sister?
She is not next to me.
Maybe she is hiding.
I call out her name.
She doesn't answer.

"I am your mother."

"I am your father."

"This is your new brother and sister."

"This is your new home."

"This is your new name."

That name is not me.
I do not want a new name.
I need to find my sister so
she can tell them I have a name.

Then the one with sparkly eyes
folds me in her arms.
"Hello. I am your grandmother.
I'm your Bubbie."
I like that name.
"When you come to my house,
I will make you chicken soup.
I make the best."

But the Bubbie doesn't live here in this house.
When she goes, the sparkly light leaves the room.

Days and days
and months go by.
Some days I cry.
But I am not allowed to cry.
I am not supposed to be sad.
I feel alone here, in this house.

I could run away.
I will take Bear too, so she won't be lonely.

I will go to Bubbie's house and we'll have chicken soup.
Nobody here hugs me like my Bubbie.

But there are places where I go, where
I love to be.
I love going to synagogue.

I love learning there.
I love laughing and playing there.

I love to be with my best friend too.
Her house is across from my house.
We talk and talk.
We ride our bikes.
We look for treasures.

Then we sit beneath the arms of the giant tree,
with leaves that flash and flutter in the sun.
I have sleepovers at her house.
I want to stay,
forever.

But the best place to be is with my Bubbie.
Anywhere my Bubbie is,
is home.
In the wintertime,
my Bubbie flies like a snowbird to where
it's summertime all the time.
"You'll come visit me in Florida."
And I do!
We talk and talk.
We listen and laugh.
We hold hands.

We look for alligators!
My Bubbie loves to hunt for alligators.
She's very brave.
"There's one!"
"AHHHH!"
I want to stay,
forever.

One day, my best friend's mom says
I am a little Cree girl.
I am? How does she know that?
But, somewhere, I know this!
I know this!
That's it! It must be!

I am a little Cree girl.
I know this, somewhere deep inside.
Every time I look at the sky.
Every time I look at myself...

I tell my father and mother,
"I am a little Cree girl."

"No. You are not."

"Yes, yes! I am!
I will tell everyone I live in a teepee!
I will break my glasses!
I will live with my Bubbie!"

"No, you will not. You are
lucky you are here. You are
lucky you always have food
and nice clothes. You are
lucky we picked your picture
from the big book."

I don't feel lucky.
I don't
I don't
I don't
belong.

I have come from somewhere else, where
I am Cree and I have a big sister
and another name.
Maybe my sister is missing me.

Years and years go by and
I run away.
I run to my Bubbie.

Knock
Knock
Knock
Her eyes sparkle when she sees me.
Her hug feels like home.

Almost every weekend,
I am with her.
We listen, we laugh, I learn.

She tells me to be kind
and to choose my words,
carefully, every day.
But then, one day, she
says, "I am not going to
be here for much longer."

I hold my Bubbie close.
Hands holding. Arms enfolding.
We are twined together
like a braid.
I am afraid.
We are afraid, together.

"You are strong. You are sunshine.
Now you are holding *me* up."
She puts her hands through my hair.
My dark hair.
And she tells me
I am beautiful.

Where will I go?
Somewhere, I have a big sister.
My Bubbie says,
"I will help you find her."

We write letters and letters.
We send them into the universe.
The universe is listening.
We find my older sister.
She has missed me,
forever.

My Bubbie sends me home.
She sends me on a big bird.
"Shalom."

One day,
I meet an Elder.
He is old and wise.
I ask him to give me my Spirit name.
"You are bright. Full of light.
You are
the Sun."
My Bubbie would love my name.
My Bubbie who made me strong.
Like the tree that reaches out its arms
and shelters everyone.

Like the Sun.
I am here.
Here.

I am Na'kuset.

A Note from Na'kuset

My Native name means "the Sun" in Mi'kmaq.

I Am My Name is a true story of my experience being adopted into a non-Indigenous family. As a Cree child, I was removed from my tribal community. A community with its own distinct government. A government that had the power to regulate our own internal affairs. It was part of the Canadian AIM program (Adopt Indian and Métis), and I was adopted by a Jewish family.

It is also the story of the transformative power of relationships.

The story is about my struggles with identity, but mostly about finding comfort, strength, and hope through my Bubbie's unconditional love. The power of this relationship between a granddaughter and grandmother is one of healing and restoration.

When I was an adult, it was my Bubbie who initiated the reunion of my biological family and led me back to my sister, Sonya, who had been searching for me since I was taken.

The bond between my sister and me was as strong as when we were children. Our reunion sustained us and inspired us to join together in initiatives to raise awareness of the Sixties Scoop and the effects of intergenerational trauma.

To the grown-ups reading along, do not underestimate the positive influence of a mentor.

You too can be that Bubbie.

A Note from Judith

I am a Bubbie. It is a name that I proudly embrace. When I see my grandchildren come running, calling out my name, I am filled with joy. And my children who embraced my mom, their Bubbie, is love passed down.

Love passed down is like a warm blanket. It is interwoven with rich histories and traditions. Of language, stories, songs, music, art. These are the threads of who you are, your identity, starting with your name.

As a child, Na'kuset never had love passed down. It was stolen from her. It was stolen from her mother and her mother before her. I had never heard of the Sixties Scoop, when Indigenous children in the 1960s were taken from their families and tribal Nations without consent. Unfortunately, this colonialist approach persists into modern day, when Indigenous children are put into foster care at much higher rates than others.

Na'kuset entrusted this story, a sacred trust, with me. And I am bound.

Embracing and sharing each other's stories is an act of truly listening, of kindness and respect. It's where we must begin, again and again. I begin with children.

I am bound to tell children.

I am that Bubbie.

A Note from Onedove

As Cree and Métis children, my mother, aunts, and uncles were scattered across two provinces, adopted and fostered by white families. It was something we only discussed in private; it carried a sense of shame. I was in my twenties when I learned about the Sixties Scoop and that my family members were survivors. I came across Na'kuset's story in 2023, and until that moment, I didn't know how widespread the forced separation of Indigenous families was. The floodgates opened and my world was shattered. Whereas before I had only heard bits and pieces about my mother's life experiences, now I learned the details—including my mother's last moment with her baby sister and brother, unaware it would be their final goodbye for many years. I reached out to Na'kuset to thank her for sharing her story, and I am forever grateful for her compassion and kindness. Her story and my mother's share a common thread, and I wanted to honor them. Throughout the pages, I have woven elements of our culture to celebrate its beauty and rich history.

*We must extend our hands and
lift everyone up.*

—*Na'kuset*

Dedicated to my sister, Sonya, and my Bubbie, who helped me find her –Na'kuset

For Miriam. Hand to heart. –J.H.

To my beloved Steven, Violet, and Ellis –Onedove

A Borzoi Book published by Alfred A. Knopf
An imprint of Random House Children's Books
A division of Penguin Random House LLC
1745 Broadway, New York, NY 10019
penguinrandomhouse.com
rhcbooks.com

Text copyright © 2025 by Na'kuset and Judith Henderson
Jacket art and interior illustrations copyright © 2025 by Chenoa Gao
Cover illustration by Chenoa Gao based on a photo by Pierre Tremblay/Listo Films

Penguin Random House values and supports copyright. Copyright fuels creativity, encourages diverse voices, promotes free speech, and creates a vibrant culture. Thank you for buying an authorized edition of this book and for complying with copyright laws by not reproducing, scanning, or distributing any part of it in any form without permission. You are supporting writers and allowing Penguin Random House to continue to publish books for every reader. Please note that no part of this book may be used or reproduced in any manner for the purpose of training artificial intelligence technologies or systems.

Knopf, Borzoi Books, and the colophon are registered trademarks of Penguin Random House LLC.

Book design by Sarah Hokanson

Library of Congress Cataloging-in-Publication Data is available upon request.
ISBN 978-0-593-64876-6 (trade) — ISBN 978-0-593-64877-3 (lib. bdg.) — ISBN 978-0-593-64878-0 (ebook)

The text of this book is set in 13-point Amasis.
The illustrations were created using a mix of traditional watercolor and digital mediums.

Manufactured in China   10 9 8 7 6 5 4 3 2 1

The authorized representative in the EU for product safety and compliance is Penguin Random House Ireland, Morrison Chambers, 32 Nassau Street, Dublin D02 YH68, Ireland, https://eu-contact.penguin.ie.

Random House Children's Books supports the First Amendment and celebrates the right to read.